Dedication :

To my wife, Katerina, and my son, Thalis

This book is dedicated to you, the two most important people in my life. Katerina, your love and support have been my constant source of strength and inspiration. You have always believed in me, even when I doubted myself. Thalis, you are my joy and my reason for living. You have taught me so much about love, laughter, and the importance of following your dreams.

This book is a testament to our love and our journey together. It is a story of hope, perseverance, and the power of believing in yourself.

I love you both more than words can express.

About the Author

I am a passionate entrepreneur, writer, and speaker. I am the founder of Limitless Passion Ltd, a company that helps people achieve their full potential online.

I am a firm believer that everyone has the potential to achieve great things. I am passionate about helping people discover their passions, set their goals, and take action to achieve their dreams.

I am also a husband and father. My wife, Katerina, and my son, Thalis, are my greatest inspirations. They are the reason I do what I do.

I hope you enjoy this book.

My Products

I offer a variety of products and services to help people achieve their goals. These include:

- Books: I have written several books on entrepreneurship, personal development, and goal setting.
- Online courses and software solutions: I offer a variety of online courses on topics such as entrepreneurship, personal development, and goal setting and softwares to automate your business online.
- Coaching: I offer one-on-one coaching to help people achieve their goals.

I am committed to helping people achieve their full potential. I believe that everyone has the ability to achieve great things.

I hope you find my products and services helpful.

Visit my blog website: https://d-papa.com/about-me

Visit my company website: https://limitlesspassionltd.com

Table of Contents

- Introduction
- Chapter 1: The Mindset of a Wealth Warrior
- Chapter 2: Unveiling Your Unique Value Proposition
- Chapter 3: Day 1: Idea Validation
- Chapter 4: Day 2: Finding Your First Customers
- Chapter 5: Beyond the Weekend: Scaling and Automating
- Chapter 6: Financial Management for Entrepreneurs
- Chapter 7: The Wealth Warrior's Journey
- Conclusion: Unleashing Your Inner Wealth Warrior

Chapter 1: The Mindset of a Wealth Warrior

Greetings, aspiring entrepreneur! Embarking on the journey toward financial independence requires more than just a brilliant idea and a weekend of hustle. It demands a mindset primed for success—the mindset of a Wealth Warrior.

In the realm of personal and professional achievement, the power of mindset cannot be overstated. It's the lens through which we view the world, the filter that shapes our thoughts, beliefs, and actions. And when it comes to entrepreneurship, the right mindset can make all the difference between fleeting dreams and tangible success.

The Psychology of Success

Successful entrepreneurs aren't a breed apart. They're not born with a special gene or bestowed with superhuman abilities. What sets them apart is their mental framework—a unique blend of attitudes, beliefs, and habits that empower them to turn dreams into reality.

They possess an unwavering belief in their vision. This isn't blind optimism; it's a deep-seated conviction that their idea has merit, that it solves a real problem, and that it can make a positive impact. This belief fuels their passion and resilience, even in the face of adversity.

They have an insatiable hunger for knowledge. Successful entrepreneurs are lifelong learners. They're constantly seeking new information, skills, and perspectives to improve themselves and their businesses. They understand that the world is constantly evolving, and to stay ahead, they must evolve too.

They exhibit a relentless drive to overcome obstacles. Entrepreneurship is rarely a smooth ride. There will be setbacks, challenges, and moments of doubt. But successful entrepreneurs don't let these obstacles deter them. They view them as opportunities for growth, learning, and innovation.

They embrace failure as a stepping stone to success. In the words of Thomas Edison, "I have not failed. I've just found 10,000 ways that won't work." Successful entrepreneurs understand that failure is not the opposite of success; it's part of the process. They learn from their mistakes, adapt their strategies, and keep moving forward.

And finally, they never give up on their goals. They have a clear vision of what they want to achieve and the tenacity to pursue it relentlessly. They understand that success rarely happens overnight. It requires consistent effort, dedication, and a willingness to weather the storms.

But here's the secret: These traits aren't innate. They're cultivated through conscious effort and practice. Anyone can develop the mindset of a Wealth Warrior. Let's delve deeper into the key strategies to make it happen.

Overcoming Limiting Beliefs and Imposter Syndrome

We all carry a backpack of limiting beliefs—those nagging voices that tell us we're not good enough, smart enough, or experienced enough to succeed. They're the remnants of past failures, societal expectations, and self-doubt that can paralyze us before we even begin.

Think back to your childhood. Perhaps you were told you weren't good at math or that you lacked artistic talent. These early experiences can shape our beliefs about ourselves and our capabilities, even years later.

Imposter syndrome is another common hurdle, particularly among high-achievers. It's that persistent feeling of being a fraud, of not deserving our accomplishments, and the fear of being exposed as inadequate.

Imagine you land your dream job or launch a successful business. Instead of feeling proud, you might feel like you're just lucky or that you're fooling everyone. You worry that at any moment, someone will discover you're not as competent as they think you are.

But these mental barriers are just that—*barriers*. They're not insurmountable. With the right tools and techniques, we can break free from their grasp and unleash our true potential.

Let's explore some strategies:

- **Challenge your negative thoughts:** When those self-limiting beliefs creep in, ask yourself, "Is this thought true? Is there evidence to support it?" Often, you'll find that these thoughts are based on fear and insecurity, not reality.
- **Reframe your perspective:** Instead of focusing on your weaknesses, shift your attention to your strengths and accomplishments. Celebrate your wins, no matter how small, and acknowledge the progress you've made.
- **Practice self-compassion:** Treat yourself with the same kindness and understanding you would offer a friend. Remember that everyone makes mistakes and experiences setbacks. It's part of the human experience.
- **Seek support from others:** Talk to trusted friends, family, or mentors about your fears and insecurities. Sharing your vulnerabilities can be

incredibly liberating and help you gain new perspectives.
- **Focus on action:** Don't let fear or self-doubt paralyze you. Take small steps every day towards your goals, even if they seem insignificant. Action breeds confidence and momentum.

Remember, overcoming limiting beliefs and imposter syndrome is an ongoing process. It requires consistent effort and a willingness to challenge your inner critic. But the rewards are immeasurable. When you break free from these mental barriers, you open yourself up to a world of possibilities.

Developing Resilience and Perseverance

The entrepreneurial journey is rarely a smooth ride. There will be setbacks, challenges, and moments of doubt. Building a thriving business requires resilience—the ability to bounce back from adversity and keep moving forward.

Think of resilience as a muscle. The more you exercise it, the stronger it becomes. Every challenge you overcome, every setback you bounce back from, builds your resilience and prepares you for the next obstacle.

Perseverance is equally crucial. It's the unwavering commitment to your goals, even when progress is slow or obstacles seem insurmountable.

Imagine you're climbing a mountain. The path is steep, the terrain is rugged, and the summit seems impossibly far away. But with each step, you get closer. You might stumble, you might fall, but you pick yourself up and keep going. That's perseverance in action.

Let's explore some techniques for cultivating resilience and perseverance:

- **Mindfulness:** Practice being present in the moment, without judgment. This can help you manage stress, regulate your emotions, and make clearer decisions.
- **Gratitude:** Focus on the things you're grateful for, even in challenging times. This can shift your perspective and foster a sense of abundance and optimism.
- **Seek support from mentors or communities:** Connect with experienced entrepreneurs or join supportive communities where you can share your struggles and learn from others.
- **Reframe setbacks as opportunities for growth:** Instead of dwelling on failures, view them as valuable learning experiences. Ask yourself, "What can I learn from this? How can I use this to improve?"
- **Develop a growth mindset:** Embrace challenges as opportunities to learn and grow.

Believe in your ability to develop new skills and overcome obstacles.
- **Set realistic expectations:** Understand that success takes time and effort. Don't expect overnight results. Focus on making progress, not perfection.
- **Celebrate your wins:** Acknowledge your accomplishments, no matter how small. This will boost your confidence and keep you motivated.
- **Take care of yourself:** Prioritize your physical and mental health. Eat well, exercise regularly, get enough sleep, and make time for activities you enjoy.

Remember, the mindset of a Wealth Warrior is not about being fearless. It's about acknowledging your fears, confronting them head-on, and taking action despite them. It's about believing in yourself, embracing challenges, and never giving up on your dreams.

As you embark on your entrepreneurial journey, keep these principles in mind. Cultivate a growth mindset, overcome limiting beliefs, and develop resilience and perseverance. With the right mindset, you can achieve anything you set your mind to. The world is waiting for your unique contribution. Go forth and make your mark!

Chapter Summary and Key Takeaways:

- The mindset of a Wealth Warrior is characterized by unwavering belief, a hunger for knowledge, a drive to overcome obstacles, an embrace of failure, and unwavering perseverance.
- Limiting beliefs and imposter syndrome are common mental barriers that can hinder success.
- Strategies for overcoming these barriers include challenging negative thoughts, reframing perspectives, practicing self-compassion, seeking support, and focusing on action.
- Resilience and perseverance are essential for navigating the challenges of entrepreneurship.
- Techniques for cultivating these qualities include mindfulness, gratitude, seeking support, reframing setbacks, developing a growth mindset, setting realistic expectations, celebrating wins, and taking care of yourself.

Actionable Steps:

- Conduct a personal SWOT analysis to identify your strengths, weaknesses, opportunities, and threats.
- Write down your limiting beliefs and challenge them with evidence and positive affirmations.

- Practice self-compassion and seek support from trusted individuals.
- Set realistic goals and break them down into smaller, actionable steps.
- Celebrate your wins and learn from your setbacks.
- Prioritize self-care and maintain a healthy work-life balance.

Remember, the journey of a thousand miles begins with a single step. Take that first step today, Wealth Warrior, and embrace the transformative power of a growth mindset.

Chapter 2: Unveiling Your Unique Value Proposition

Welcome back, Wealth Warrior! We've fortified our mindset and are ready to roll up our sleeves and get down to business. But before we dive into the 48-hour action plan, we need to uncover the cornerstone of your entrepreneurial venture: your unique value proposition.

Think of your value proposition as your business's North Star—it's the guiding light that illuminates your path, differentiates you from the competition, and attracts your ideal customers. It's the essence of what you offer, the problem you solve, and the transformation you provide.

In this chapter, we'll embark on a journey of self-discovery and market exploration. We'll delve into your strengths, weaknesses, opportunities, and threats, identify your ideal target audience, and craft a compelling value proposition that resonates with their deepest desires.

Step-by-Step Guide to Conducting a Personal SWOT Analysis

A personal SWOT analysis is a powerful tool for gaining clarity on your internal and external landscape. It helps you leverage your strengths, address your weaknesses, seize opportunities, and mitigate threats. Here's how to conduct one:

1. **Strengths:** What are you naturally good at? What skills and experiences do you possess? What resources or connections do you have access to? Perhaps you're a gifted writer, a skilled programmer, or a natural salesperson. Maybe you have a network of industry contacts or access to specialized equipment. Identifying your strengths allows you to capitalize on your unique talents and resources.

2. **Weaknesses:** What areas do you need to improve in? What tasks or activities do you struggle with? What limitations or constraints do you face? Maybe you're not tech-savvy, or you struggle with time management. Recognizing your weaknesses allows you to develop strategies to address them, whether through learning new skills, seeking help from others, or outsourcing tasks.

3. **Opportunities:** What trends or market gaps can you capitalize on? What emerging technologies or platforms can you leverage? What potential partnerships or collaborations can you explore? The world is constantly changing, and with change comes opportunity. A growth mindset allows you to spot these opportunities and seize them.

4. **Threats:** What obstacles or challenges might you encounter? What are your competitors doing well? What economic or industry-specific factors could impact your business? It's important to be realistic about the potential threats you might face. This doesn't mean dwelling on negativity, but rather proactively identifying potential challenges and developing strategies to mitigate them.

Exercises to Identify Your Ideal Target Audience

Your ideal target audience is the group of people who are most likely to benefit from your product or service. They're the ones who will eagerly pay for your solution and become your loyal customers. To identify them, consider the following:

- **Demographics:** Age, gender, location, income level, education level, occupation, etc. These basic demographic factors can help you paint a picture of your ideal customer.
- **Psychographics:** Interests, values, beliefs, lifestyle, personality traits, etc. Understanding your target audience's psychographics allows you to connect with them on a deeper level and tailor your messaging to their specific needs and desires.
- **Pain Points:** What problems or challenges do they face? What are their unmet needs or desires? By understanding their pain points,

you can position your product or service as the solution they've been searching for.
- **Aspirations:** What goals or dreams do they have? What transformation do they seek? By tapping into their aspirations, you can create a compelling value proposition that inspires them to take action.

Remember, the more specific you can be about your target audience, the more effective your marketing and messaging will be. Don't try to please everyone—focus on serving a niche and becoming the go-to solution for their specific needs.

Examples of Compelling Value Propositions Across Different Industries

A strong value proposition is clear, concise, and speaks directly to your target audience's pain points and aspirations. Here are a few examples from different industries to inspire you:

- **Health and Wellness:** "Transform your body and mind with our personalized fitness and nutrition plans, designed to help you achieve your health goals and feel your best."
- **Education and E-learning:** "Unlock your full potential with our online courses, taught by industry experts, and gain the skills you need to succeed in today's competitive job market."
- **Technology and SaaS:** "Streamline your workflow and boost productivity with our

cloud-based software, designed to automate repetitive tasks and save you valuable time."
- **Finance and Investing:** "Achieve financial freedom and build a secure future with our comprehensive investment strategies, tailored to your risk tolerance and financial goals."
- **Creative Arts:** "Unleash your creativity and express yourself with our online art classes, led by experienced instructors, and discover the joy of artistic expression."
- **Home and Lifestyle:** "Create a beautiful and functional living space with our curated collection of home decor and organization solutions, designed to simplify your life and elevate your style."
- **Pet Care:** "Pamper your furry friend with our all-natural pet products, made with love and care, and give them the happy and healthy life they deserve."
- **Travel and Hospitality:** "Experience unforgettable adventures and create lasting memories with our personalized travel itineraries and curated experiences, designed to cater to your unique interests and preferences."

Remember, these are just examples. Your unique value proposition will depend on your specific business idea and target audience. Take the time to craft a message that truly resonates with your ideal customers and clearly communicates the transformation you offer.

The Growth Mindset in Crafting Your Value Proposition

As you craft your value proposition, remember that a growth mindset embraces feedback and iteration. Don't be afraid to test different versions of your message and gather feedback from your target audience. See what resonates, what doesn't, and refine your value proposition accordingly.

Remember, your value proposition is not set in stone. It can evolve and adapt as your business grows and your understanding of your customers deepens. Embrace the process of continuous improvement, and your value proposition will become a powerful tool for attracting and retaining loyal customers.

Chapter Summary and Key Takeaways

- Your unique value proposition is the cornerstone of your entrepreneurial venture. It differentiates you from the competition and attracts your ideal customers.
- A personal SWOT analysis helps you leverage your strengths, address your weaknesses, scize opportunities, and mitigate threats.
- Identifying your ideal target audience involves understanding their demographics, psychographics, pain points, and aspirations.

- A compelling value proposition is clear, concise, and speaks directly to your target audience's needs and desires.
- Embrace a growth mindset when crafting your value proposition, seeking feedback and iterating to ensure it resonates with your ideal customers.

Actionable Steps:

- Conduct a personal SWOT analysis.
- Create a detailed profile of your ideal target audience.
- Brainstorm and test different versions of your value proposition.
- Gather feedback from your target audience and refine your message accordingly.
- Use your value proposition to guide your marketing and messaging efforts.

By the end of this chapter, you should have a crystal-clear understanding of your unique value proposition and how it sets you apart from the competition. You'll have identified your ideal customer and crafted a compelling message that speaks directly to their needs and desires. With this foundation in place, you'll be ready to launch your 6-figure side hustle in just 48 hours. So, let's get started!

Chapter 3: Day 1: Idea Validation

Welcome to Day 1, Wealth Warriors! Today, we shift gears from self-discovery and market exploration to action. It's time to put your ideas to the test and validate their potential in the real world.

Remember, a brilliant idea is only as good as its execution. And the foundation of successful execution is ensuring there's a genuine need and demand for what you're offering.

In this chapter, we'll embrace a growth mindset, roll up our sleeves, and dive into the practical steps of idea validation. We'll brainstorm and narrow down your business concepts, conduct thorough market research, and create a simple yet effective landing page or survey to gauge interest.

Embracing the Growth Mindset in Idea Validation

Before we dive into the practical steps, let's revisit the power of a growth mindset in this crucial phase.

In a fixed mindset, idea validation can feel like a high-stakes test. You might cling to your initial idea, fearing failure or rejection. You might hesitate to seek feedback, worried that it will expose flaws or weaknesses.

But in a growth mindset, idea validation is an opportunity for learning, iteration, and refinement. It's a chance to gather valuable data, identify potential pitfalls, and make informed decisions that increase your chances of success.

Remember, the goal isn't to prove your idea is perfect from the start. It's to test your assumptions, challenge your biases, and gather evidence to support (or disprove) your hypothesis. It's about embracing the process of discovery and being open to adjusting your course along the way.

Brainstorming and Narrowing Down Business Ideas

If you're brimming with ideas, that's fantastic! But for our 48-hour sprint, we need to focus. Start by brainstorming a list of potential business ideas, keeping your value proposition and target audience in mind.

Let your creativity flow. Don't censor yourself or dismiss any idea too quickly. Write down everything that comes to mind, no matter how wild or impractical it might seem at first.

Once you have a list, it's time to evaluate each idea based on a set of criteria. This is where your growth mindset shines. Be objective, critical, and willing to let go of ideas that don't meet the mark.

Consider the following factors:

- **Market demand:** Is there a genuine need for this product or service? Does it solve a real problem or fulfill a desire for your target audience?
- **Profit potential:** Can you generate sustainable revenue? Are there enough people willing to pay for your solution at a price that allows you to make a profit?
- **Personal passion:** Are you genuinely excited about this idea? Will you be motivated to work on it even when faced with challenges?
- **Feasibility:** Can you realistically launch and execute this within a weekend? Do you have the necessary skills, resources, and time to bring this idea to life?

Remember, a growth mindset encourages experimentation. Don't be afraid to let go of ideas that don't meet the criteria and focus on the ones with the highest potential for success.

Conducting Market Research and Competitor Analysis

Now it's time to roll up your sleeves and dig deeper into your chosen ideas. Market research helps you understand your target audience's pain points, preferences, and behaviors. Competitor analysis reveals what's already out there and how you can differentiate yourself.

Think of market research as a conversation with your potential customers. You're listening to their needs, understanding their challenges, and uncovering their desires.

Utilize a variety of resources to gather insights:

- **Online surveys and questionnaires:** Create targeted surveys to gather quantitative and qualitative data from your target audience.
- **Social media listening:** Monitor conversations and hashtags relevant to your industry or niche to understand what people are talking about and what their pain points are.
- **Keyword research:** Use tools like Google Keyword Planner to identify popular search terms related to your business idea, revealing potential demand and competition.
- **Industry reports and publications:** Stay informed about industry trends, forecasts, and consumer behavior through reputable sources.
- **Direct conversations with potential customers:** Reach out to people in your target audience and ask open-ended questions to gain deeper insights.

Remember, feedback is a gift, even if it's not what you want to hear. A growth mindset welcomes constructive criticism as an opportunity for improvement.

Creating a Simple Landing Page or Survey to Gauge Interest

A landing page or survey is a quick and effective way to test your idea and gauge market interest. Use a simple website builder or survey tool to create a basic page that outlines your value proposition and invites visitors to take action (e.g., sign up for a waitlist, express interest, provide feedback).

Focus on clarity and simplicity. Your landing page or survey should be easy to understand and navigate. Highlight the key benefits of your product or service and make it clear what action you want visitors to take.

Share your landing page or survey on social media, relevant online communities, and with your personal network. Monitor the responses and analyze the data to gain valuable insights into your target audience's level of interest and their specific needs.

Remember, the goal is not to create a perfect landing page or survey. It's to get your idea in front of potential customers and gather feedback. Embrace the iterative process and be willing to make adjustments based on what you learn.

Embracing Feedback and Iterating

As you gather feedback, be open to adjusting your idea or approach. A growth mindset sees challenges as opportunities for learning and improvement. Don't be afraid to pivot or iterate based on what you discover.

Remember, the goal of Day 1 is to validate your idea and ensure there's a genuine need and demand for what you're offering. By the end of the day, you should have a clear understanding of your target audience, their pain points, and their willingness to pay for your solution.

With this valuable knowledge in hand, you'll be ready to hit the ground running on Day 2, where we'll focus on finding your first customers and making those initial sales. So, embrace the growth mindset, gather your data, and let's get ready to turn your idea into a reality!

Chapter Summary and Key Takeaways

- Idea validation is a crucial step in the entrepreneurial process, ensuring there's a genuine need and demand for your product or service.
- A growth mindset views idea validation as an opportunity for learning, iteration, and refinement.
- Brainstorming and narrowing down business ideas involves evaluating each idea based on market demand, profit potential, personal passion, and feasibility.

- Conducting market research and competitor analysis helps you understand your target audience and differentiate yourself from the competition.
- Creating a simple landing page or survey allows you to test your idea and gauge market interest.
- Embracing feedback and iterating is key to refining your idea and increasing your chances of success.

Actionable Steps:

- Brainstorm a list of potential business ideas.
- Evaluate each idea based on the criteria discussed in the chapter.
- Conduct market research and competitor analysis.
- Create a simple landing page or survey.
- Share your landing page or survey and gather feedback.
- Analyze the feedback and iterate on your idea as needed.

By following these steps and embracing a growth mindset, you'll be well on your way to validating your idea and building a successful business. Remember, every successful entrepreneur started with an idea. Now it's your turn to turn your idea into a reality!

Chapter 4: Day 2: Finding Your First Customers

Welcome to Day 2, Wealth Warriors! Today, the rubber meets the road. We're shifting from idea validation to action, from theory to practice. It's time to find your first customers and make those initial sales.

Remember, a growth mindset views challenges as opportunities for learning and improvement. Don't be afraid to experiment, adapt, and refine your approach based on the feedback you receive. Today is about taking bold steps, putting yourself out there, and connecting with your target audience.

In-Depth Strategies for Leveraging Various Social Media Platforms

Social media is a powerful tool for reaching and engaging with your target audience. It's a bustling marketplace of ideas, conversations, and connections, waiting for you to tap into its potential.

But with so many platforms available, it's essential to focus your efforts where your ideal customers spend their time. Let's explore some in-depth strategies for leveraging various social media platforms:

- **Facebook:**
    - **Create a compelling business page:** Your Facebook business page is your

virtual storefront. Make sure it's visually appealing, informative, and reflects your brand identity.
- **Share valuable content:** Post engaging content that resonates with your target audience. This could include blog posts, articles, videos, infographics, or even live streams.
- **Engage in relevant groups and communities:** Join groups and communities where your ideal customers hang out. Participate in discussions, offer valuable insights, and build relationships.
- **Run targeted ads:** Facebook's advertising platform allows you to reach a highly specific audience based on demographics, interests, and behaviors. Consider running ads to promote your product or service, drive traffic to your landing page, or generate leads.

- **Instagram:**
  - **Focus on visually appealing content:** Instagram is all about aesthetics. Make sure your photos and videos are high-quality, eye-catching, and relevant to your brand.
  - **Utilize relevant hashtags:** Hashtags help people discover your content. Research

popular hashtags in your niche and use them strategically in your posts.
- **Engage with your followers:** Respond to comments, answer questions, and participate in conversations. Building relationships with your followers is key to fostering loyalty and trust.
- **Partner with influencers:** Identify influencers in your niche who have a strong following and align with your brand values. Collaborate with them to reach a wider audience and gain credibility.

- **Twitter:**
  - **Share concise and informative tweets:** Twitter's character limit forces you to be concise. Craft tweets that are informative, engaging, and spark conversations.
  - **Participate in relevant Twitter chats:** Twitter chats are live discussions around a specific topic or hashtag. They're a great way to connect with potential customers, industry leaders, and other entrepreneurs.
  - **Engage with industry leaders and potential customers:** Retweet their content, reply to their tweets, and participate in conversations. Building

relationships with influential people in your industry can open doors and create opportunities.

- **LinkedIn:**

    - **Build a professional profile:** Your LinkedIn profile is your online resume. Make sure it's complete, up-to-date, and showcases your skills and experience.
    - **Connect with potential customers and partners:** LinkedIn is a powerful networking platform. Connect with people in your industry, engage in conversations, and build relationships.
    - **Share thought leadership content:** Position yourself as an expert in your field by sharing valuable insights and perspectives. This can help you attract potential customers and partners.
    - **Participate in relevant groups and discussions:** Join groups and discussions relevant to your industry or niche. Share your expertise, ask questions, and connect with other professionals.

- **TikTok:**

    - **Create short, engaging videos:** TikTok is all about short-form video content. Create videos that are fun, creative, and

showcase your product or service in a unique way.
- **Use trending sounds and challenges:** Tap into popular trends and challenges to increase your reach and engagement.
- **Collaborate with other creators:** Partner with other TikTok creators to cross-promote your content and reach new audiences.

Remember, authenticity and consistency are key on social media. Be yourself, provide value, and engage with your audience genuinely. Building a strong social media presence takes time and effort, but it's a valuable investment in your business's growth.

Scripts or Templates for Reaching Out to Potential Customers and Partners

Reaching out to potential customers and partners can be intimidating, but it's a crucial step in building your business. It's about initiating conversations, building relationships, and creating opportunities.

Here are some scripts or templates to help you get started:

Email Template for Potential Customers:

Subject: [Your Business Name] - Helping you achieve [Desired Outcome]

Hi [Name],

I hope this email finds you well.

I noticed that you're interested in [Pain Point or Interest]. I'm reaching out because I believe my product/service, [Your Product/Service Name], can help you [Solve Problem or Achieve Goal].

Here's how it works: [Briefly explain your product/service and its key benefits].

I'd love to chat more about how [Your Product/Service Name] can help you. Are you available for a quick call sometime this week?

Best regards, [Your Name]

LinkedIn Message Template for Potential Partners:

Hi [Name],

I came across your profile and was impressed by your work in [Industry or Niche]. I'm the founder of [Your Business Name], and we're also passionate about [Shared Interest or Goal].

I believe there could be a potential synergy between our businesses. I'd love to connect and explore opportunities for collaboration.

Would you be open to a brief chat sometime this week?

Best regards, [Your Name]

Remember to personalize your outreach messages. Tailor them to the specific recipient and their needs. Show that you've done your research and that you genuinely care about helping them.

Offer Guidance on Creating Compelling Offers and Promotions

To entice your first customers, consider creating irresistible offers and promotions. These are incentives that make your product or service more appealing and encourage people to take action.

Here are some ideas:

- **Limited-time discounts:** Offer a discount for a limited time to create a sense of urgency. This can be especially effective during launch periods or special events.
- **Early-bird pricing:** Offer a special price for the first few customers to incentivize early adoption. This rewards those who take action quickly and helps you build initial momentum.
- **Bundle deals:** Package multiple products or services together at a discounted price. This provides added value to customers and encourages them to purchase more.

- **Free trials or consultations:** Offer a free trial or consultation to allow potential customers to experience your product or service risk-free. This builds trust and confidence in your offering.
- **Referral programs:** Encourage existing customers to refer their friends and family in exchange for a discount or reward. This leverages the power of word-of-mouth marketing and helps you expand your reach.

Remember, your offers and promotions should be aligned with your value proposition and target audience. Focus on highlighting the benefits and transformation your product or service provides.

Chapter Summary and Key Takeaways

- Day 2 is all about taking action and finding your first customers.
- Social media is a powerful tool for reaching and engaging with your target audience.
- Personalize your outreach messages and tailor them to the specific recipient.
- Create compelling offers and promotions to entice your first customers.
- Embrace a growth mindset and be willing to experiment and adapt your approach.

Actionable Steps

- Choose the social media platforms where your ideal customers spend their time.
- Create engaging content and participate in relevant conversations.
- Reach out to potential customers and partners with personalized messages.
- Craft irresistible offers and promotions.
- Track your results and refine your approach based on feedback.

Remember, finding your first customers is a crucial milestone in your entrepreneurial journey. It validates your idea, provides valuable feedback, and sets the stage for future growth. Embrace the challenge, stay persistent, and celebrate every win along the way. You're building something special, Wealth Warrior!

Chapter 5: Beyond the Weekend: Scaling and Automating

Congratulations, Wealth Warrior! You've successfully navigated the initial hurdles of entrepreneurship. You've validated your idea, found your first customers, and made those crucial initial sales. Now, it's time to look beyond the weekend and lay the groundwork for sustainable growth and scalability.

Remember, a growth mindset views success not as a destination but as a continuous journey of learning and improvement. As your business expands, you'll encounter new challenges and opportunities. Embrace them with enthusiasm, adaptability, and a relentless pursuit of progress.

Building a Strong Brand and Online Presence

In today's digital age, a strong brand and online presence are essential for any business, especially for those operating primarily or exclusively online. Your brand represents your identity, values, and the promise you make to your customers. It's what sets you apart from the competition and fosters trust, loyalty, and recognition.

Think of your brand as your business's personality. It's how you communicate who you are, what you stand for, and what makes you unique. A strong brand creates an emotional connection with your audience, builds credibility, and makes your business memorable.

Your online presence encompasses your website, social media profiles, email marketing, and any other digital channels you use to connect with your audience. It's your virtual storefront, where potential customers can learn about your product or service, interact with your brand, and make purchases.

Investing time and effort in creating a cohesive and compelling brand identity that reflects your values and resonates with your target audience is paramount. Ensure your online presence is user-friendly, visually appealing, and optimized for conversions.

Remember, building a strong brand takes time and consistency. But it's an investment that will pay off in the long run as it helps you attract and retain loyal customers, increase brand recognition, and ultimately drive sales.

Recommended Tools and Resources for Automation and Outsourcing

As your business grows, you'll likely find yourself overwhelmed with tasks and responsibilities. It's natural to feel stretched thin as you juggle customer inquiries, marketing efforts, product development, and countless other aspects of running a business.

That's where automation and outsourcing come in. By leveraging technology and delegating tasks, you can free up your time to focus on strategic activities that drive growth, innovation, and long-term success.

Here are some recommended tools and resources to help you streamline your operations and scale your business:

- **Customer Relationship Management (CRM):** Salesforce, HubSpot, Zoho CRM. These powerful tools help you manage customer interactions, track leads, and nurture relationships, ensuring no opportunity slips through the cracks.

- **Email Marketing:** Mailchimp, ConvertKit, ActiveCampaign. Email marketing remains a highly effective way to connect with your audience, nurture leads, and drive sales. These platforms offer automation features, customizable templates, and analytics to track your results.

- **Social Media Management:** Hootsuite, Buffer, Sprout Social. Managing multiple social media accounts can be time-consuming. These tools allow you to schedule posts, monitor conversations, and track engagement across various platforms from a single dashboard.

- **Project Management:** Asana, Trello, Monday.com. As your team and projects grow, staying organized is crucial. Project management tools help you track tasks, collaborate with team members, and ensure deadlines are met.

- **E-commerce Platforms:** Shopify, WooCommerce, BigCommerce. If you're selling products online, a robust e-commerce platform is essential. These platforms offer customizable storefronts, secure payment processing, and inventory management tools.

- **Payment Processing:** Stripe, PayPal, Square. Accepting payments online should be seamless and secure. These payment processors offer easy integration with your website or e-commerce platform and handle various payment methods.

- **Outsourcing Platforms:** Upwork, Fiverr, Freelancer. When you need specialized skills or additional manpower, outsourcing platforms connect you with talented freelancers from around the world.

Remember, choose tools and resources that align with your business needs and budget. Start with the essentials and gradually add more as your business expands. Don't be afraid to experiment and find what works best for you.

Tips for Managing Customer Relationships and Providing Excellent Support

Happy customers are the lifeblood of any successful business. They're more likely to make repeat purchases, refer their friends and family, and leave positive reviews, all of which contribute to your long-term growth.

Prioritizing customer relationship management and providing excellent support is key to building a loyal customer base and fostering a positive brand reputation.

Here are some tips to cultivate strong customer relationships:

- **Respond promptly to inquiries and feedback:** Acknowledge customer messages and comments quickly and professionally. Show that you value their time and input.

- **Personalize your interactions:** Use customers' names and reference their previous purchases or interactions to show you care and that they're not just another number.

- **Go the extra mile:** Exceed customer expectations by offering surprise discounts, personalized recommendations, or handwritten thank-you notes. These small gestures can make a big difference in building loyalty and goodwill.

- **Create a loyalty program:** Reward repeat customers with exclusive discounts, early access to new products, or special events. This incentivizes them to continue doing business with you.

- **Actively seek feedback:** Encourage customers to share their thoughts and suggestions, and use their feedback to improve your product or service. Show that you're listening and that you value their input.

Remember, building strong customer relationships is an ongoing process. It requires consistent effort, genuine empathy, and a commitment to providing exceptional service.

Chapter Summary and Key Takeaways

- Scaling your business requires a shift in focus from initial validation to sustainable growth and automation.
- Building a strong brand and online presence is essential for establishing credibility, attracting customers, and fostering loyalty.

- Leveraging technology and outsourcing can free up your time and allow you to focus on strategic activities that drive growth.
- Prioritizing customer relationship management and providing excellent support are crucial for building a loyal customer base and positive brand reputation.
- Embrace a growth mindset and view challenges as opportunities to learn and improve.

Actionable Steps:

- Define your brand identity and create a cohesive brand message.
- Develop a user-friendly and visually appealing website.
- Establish a strong presence on relevant social media platforms.
- Identify tasks that can be automated or outsourced and implement appropriate tools and resources.
- Prioritize customer satisfaction and actively seek feedback to improve your product or service.

By following these strategies and embracing a growth mindset, you'll be well on your way to scaling your business and achieving long-term success. Remember, the journey is just beginning. Stay curious, keep learning, and never stop striving for improvement. You have the potential to build something truly extraordinary.

Chapter 6: Financial Management for Entrepreneurs

Welcome, Wealth Warriors, to the realm of numbers and financial savvy! As your business grows, mastering financial management becomes paramount. It's time to ditch any fear of spreadsheets and embrace the empowering role of numbers in your entrepreneurial journey.

Remember, a growth mindset views financial literacy as a skill to be developed, not a burden to be avoided. Let's demystify the basics and equip you with the knowledge to make informed decisions that fuel your business's growth.

Explain Basic Accounting Principles in an Accessible Way

Accounting might seem intimidating, conjuring images of complex ledgers and confusing jargon. But at its core, it's simply the process of tracking your income and expenses. Think of it as your business's financial diary, recording every transaction and providing a clear picture of your financial health.

Just as a personal diary helps you reflect on your experiences and make better choices, accounting helps you understand your business's financial journey and make informed decisions that lead to growth and profitability.

Let's break down some key accounting principles in a way that's easy to understand:

- **Revenue:** This is the money your business earns from selling your products or services. It's the lifeblood of your business, fueling its operations and growth.

- **Expenses:** These are the costs you incur to run your business. They can be fixed costs, like rent and salaries, or variable costs, like marketing expenses and inventory. Managing your expenses effectively is crucial for maintaining profitability.

- **Assets:** These are things your business owns that have value. They can be tangible assets, like cash, inventory, equipment, and property, or intangible assets, like intellectual property and brand recognition. Your assets represent your business's resources and potential for future growth.

- **Liabilities:** These are debts or obligations your business owes. They can be short-term liabilities, like accounts payable and accrued expenses, or long-term liabilities, like loans and mortgages. Understanding your liabilities is essential for managing your cash flow and making sound financial decisions.

- **Equity:** This represents the owner's investment in the business and the accumulated profits (or losses). It's the residual interest in the assets of the business after deducting liabilities. Equity reflects the net worth of your business and your ownership stake.

By diligently tracking these elements, you can generate crucial financial statements like:

- **The Balance Sheet:** A snapshot of your business's financial position at a specific point in time, showing your assets, liabilities, and equity.
- **The Income Statement:** A summary of your business's revenues and expenses over a specific period, revealing your net income or loss.
- **The Cash Flow Statement:** A report of your business's cash inflows and outflows during a specific period, providing insights into your liquidity and ability to meet financial obligations.

These financial statements are like your business's vital signs, providing valuable information about its overall health and performance. By regularly reviewing and analyzing these statements, you can identify trends, make informed decisions, and proactively manage your finances.

Offer Guidance on Choosing the Right Business Structure

Selecting the right business structure is a critical decision with legal and tax implications. It's like choosing the foundation for your entrepreneurial house. A solid foundation provides stability and protection, while a weak one can lead to cracks and instability.

Let's explore a few common business structures:

- **Sole Proprietorship:** This is the simplest and most common structure, where you and your business are considered one entity. It's easy to set up and offers maximum control, but it also comes with unlimited personal liability, meaning your personal assets are at risk if your business faces legal or financial trouble.

- **Partnership:** A partnership is a business owned by two or more people who share profits and liabilities. It offers shared responsibility and resources, but it also comes with unlimited liability for each partner.

- **Limited Liability Company (LLC):** An LLC offers personal liability protection, meaning your personal assets are generally shielded from business debts and lawsuits. It also provides flexibility in taxation, allowing you to choose between being taxed as a partnership or a corporation.

- **Corporation:** A corporation is a separate legal entity from its owners, offering the strongest liability protection. However, it's also the most complex structure, with more regulations, formalities, and potential double taxation.

Choosing the right business structure depends on various factors, such as the nature of your business, your risk tolerance, your tax situation, and your long-term goals. It's essential to consult with a legal or financial professional to understand the pros and cons of each option and make an informed decision that aligns with your specific circumstances.

Remember, a growth mindset welcomes seeking expert advice. It's not a sign of weakness but rather a proactive approach to mitigating risks and setting your business up for success.

Provide Tips for Budgeting, Saving, and Investing for Future Growth

Financial planning is the compass that guides your business toward sustainable growth and long-term success. It's about creating a roadmap for your financial journey, anticipating challenges, and seizing opportunities.

Here are some essential tips to help you navigate the financial landscape:

- **Create a budget:** A budget is your financial blueprint. It outlines your expected income and expenses, helping you track your spending, identify areas for savings, and make informed decisions about resource allocation.

- **Set financial goals:** Define clear and measurable financial goals for your business. These goals could include reaching a certain revenue target, achieving profitability, or securing funding for expansion. Having specific goals provides focus and direction for your financial planning.

- **Build an emergency fund:** Unexpected expenses and economic downturns can happen to any business. An emergency fund, typically 3-6 months of operating expenses, provides a safety net to weather these storms and maintain financial stability.

- **Invest in your business:** To grow your business, you need to invest in it. Allocate funds for marketing, product development, hiring talented team members, and other initiatives that drive growth and innovation.

- **Diversify your investments:** Don't put all your eggs in one basket. Consider investing in a variety of assets, such as stocks, bonds, real estate, or other ventures, to spread your risk and create multiple streams of income.

- **Seek professional guidance:** If you're unsure about financial matters, don't hesitate to seek help from a financial advisor or accountant. They can provide valuable insights, help you create a sound financial plan, and ensure you're making the most of your resources.

Remember, financial management is an ongoing process. It requires discipline, adaptability, and a willingness to learn and grow. Regularly review your budget, track your progress toward your goals, and adjust your strategies as needed. A growth mindset views challenges as opportunities to refine your financial skills and make even better decisions.

By mastering financial management, you'll gain confidence, make informed decisions, and pave the way for sustainable growth. Remember, financial success is not about accumulating wealth for its own sake. It's about creating opportunities, achieving your goals, and making a positive impact on the world. So, embrace the numbers, Wealth Warrior, and let them fuel your journey to extraordinary success!

Chapter Summary and Key Takeaways

- Financial management is crucial for the sustainable growth and success of your business
- Understanding basic accounting principles, such as revenue, expenses, assets, liabilities, and equity, helps you track your financial health and make informed decisions.
- Choosing the right business structure is a critical decision with legal and tax implications. Consult with a professional to determine the best option for your specific circumstances.
- Financial planning, including budgeting, setting goals, building an emergency fund, and investing in your business, is essential for long-term success.
- A growth mindset views financial literacy as a skill to be developed, not a burden to be avoided. Embrace challenges, seek expert advice, and continuously refine your financial strategies.

Actionable Steps:

- Set up a basic accounting system to track your income and expenses.
- Consult with a legal or financial professional to choose the right business structure.

- Create a budget and track your spending regularly.
- Define clear financial goals for your business.
- Start building an emergency fund.
- Allocate funds for marketing, product development, and other growth initiatives.
- Consider diversifying your investments to spread risk and create multiple income streams.
- Regularly review your financial statements and adjust your strategies as needed.
- Seek professional guidance if you have any questions or concerns.

By taking these actionable steps and embracing a growth mindset, you'll empower yourself to make sound financial decisions, navigate challenges with confidence, and build a thriving and sustainable business. Remember, financial mastery is not an overnight achievement; it's a continuous journey of learning and growth.

Chapter 7: The Wealth Warrior's Journey

Congratulations, Wealth Warrior! You've journeyed through mindset mastery, idea validation, customer acquisition, scaling strategies, and financial acumen. Now, as we approach the final chapter, let's celebrate your progress and look ahead to the exciting path that lies before you.

The entrepreneurial journey is a lifelong adventure, filled with twists, turns, triumphs, and setbacks. It's a testament to the human spirit's resilience, creativity, and unwavering pursuit of dreams. It's a path forged by those who dare to challenge the status quo, embrace uncertainty, and create their own destinies.

Stories and Case Studies of Successful Entrepreneurs

Let's draw inspiration from those who have walked the path before us. From humble beginnings to remarkable achievements, their stories remind us that anything is possible with passion, perseverance, and a growth mindset.

- **The Accidental Tech Mogul:** Imagine a young woman, fresh out of college, working a dead-end job she despised. Frustrated and yearning for more, she started tinkering with code in her spare time, building a simple app to solve a problem she faced. Little did she know that this side project would evolve into a multi-million dollar tech company, revolutionizing an entire industry.

- **The Community Builder Turned Social Entrepreneur:** Picture a passionate advocate for social justice, driven by a desire to make a difference in the world. With limited resources but boundless determination, they started a grassroots movement, connecting people, raising awareness, and sparking change. Their efforts grew into a thriving social enterprise, empowering communities and creating a sustainable impact.

- **The Culinary Artist Who Spiced Up the Food Scene:** Envision a home cook with a flair for flavor and a dream to share their culinary creations with the world. Starting with a small catering business from their own kitchen, they experimented, iterated, and perfected their recipes. Through word-of-mouth and social media buzz, their business blossomed into a beloved local restaurant, delighting taste buds and inspiring others to pursue their passions.

These stories, and countless others like them, demonstrate the boundless possibilities that await those who dare to dream big and take action. They showcase the transformative power of entrepreneurship, not just in terms of financial success but also in terms of personal growth, fulfillment, and making a meaningful contribution to the world.

Tips for Maintaining Motivation and Staying Focused

The entrepreneurial journey can be exhilarating, but it's not without its challenges. There will be moments of doubt, setbacks, and the temptation to give up. It's during these tough times that your mindset and resilience will be truly tested.

Here are some tips to help you stay motivated and focused, even when the going gets tough:

- **Set Clear Goals and Visualize Your Success:** Define what you want to achieve and create a vivid mental picture of your desired outcome. Write down your goals, create vision boards, or use visualization techniques to keep your aspirations front and center. The more clarity you have about your goals, the easier it will be to stay motivated and focused.

- **Break Down Big Goals into Smaller, Actionable Steps:** Overwhelming goals can lead to procrastination and discouragement. Break them down into smaller, more manageable tasks. This makes them less intimidating and provides a sense of progress as you complete each step.

- **Surround Yourself with Positive and Supportive People:** Connect with like-minded individuals who believe in your vision and encourage your growth. Seek out mentors, join entrepreneurial communities, and surround yourself with people who uplift and inspire you. Avoid negative influences that drain your energy and enthusiasm.

- **Celebrate Your Wins, No Matter How Small:** Acknowledge your progress and achievements, even if they seem insignificant. Every step forward is a victory worth celebrating. This will boost your confidence, reinforce positive habits, and keep you motivated to continue pushing forward.

- **Practice Self-Care and Prioritize Your Well-being:** The entrepreneurial journey can be demanding, both physically and mentally. Take breaks, exercise, eat healthy, and get enough sleep. Make time for activities you enjoy and that recharge your batteries. Remember, a healthy mind and body are essential for peak performance and sustained motivation.

- **Embrace a Growth Mindset and Learn from Setbacks:** Setbacks and failures are inevitable. But a growth mindset views these challenges as opportunities for learning and improvement. Analyze what went wrong, extract valuable lessons, and use those insights to refine your approach and make better decisions in the future.

- **Cultivate Gratitude and Focus on the Positive:** Take time each day to reflect on the things you're grateful for. This practice can shift your perspective, foster a sense of abundance, and help you stay focused on the positive aspects of your journey, even during challenging times.

- **Find Your "Why" and Connect with Your Purpose:** What drives you? What impact do you want to make in the world? Connecting with your deeper purpose can provide a powerful source of motivation and resilience, especially when faced with obstacles.

Remember, motivation is not a constant state. It ebbs and flows. But by cultivating healthy habits, surrounding yourself with positivity, and connecting with your purpose, you can weather the storms and stay focused on your long-term vision.

Encouragement to Continue Learning and Growing

The world is constantly changing, and so too must we. A growth mindset thrives on continuous learning and development. Embrace new challenges, seek out knowledge and skills, and never stop evolving.

Here are some ways to foster a lifelong learning mindset:

- **Read Books, Articles, and Blogs:** Stay informed about industry trends, new technologies, and best practices. Expand your knowledge base and gain fresh perspectives by reading widely and diversely.

- **Attend Workshops, Conferences, and Webinars:** Network with other entrepreneurs, learn from experts in your field, and stay abreast of the latest developments in your industry. These events offer valuable opportunities for learning, collaboration, and inspiration.

- **Take Online Courses or Pursue Formal Education:** Whether you're interested in acquiring new skills, deepening your expertise, or exploring a new field, online courses and formal education programs provide structured learning experiences that can accelerate your growth.

- **Seek Out Mentors and Advisors:** Connect with experienced individuals who can offer guidance, support, and valuable insights based on their own journeys. A mentor can provide a sounding board for your ideas, offer constructive feedback, and help you navigate challenges.

- **Experiment and Embrace Failure as a Learning Opportunity:** Don't be afraid to try new things and step outside your comfort zone. Experiment with different strategies, test new ideas, and embrace failure as a natural part of the learning process. Extract valuable lessons from your mistakes and use them to fuel your growth.

- **Cultivate Curiosity and a Thirst for Knowledge:** Approach every experience with a sense of curiosity and wonder. Ask questions, seek answers, and never stop exploring. The more you learn, the more equipped you'll be to adapt, innovate, and thrive in an ever-changing world.

Remember, the journey of a Wealth Warrior is one of continuous evolution. Embrace the challenges, celebrate the victories, and never stop striving for your full potential. The world is waiting for your unique contribution. Go forth and make your mark!

Chapter Summary and Key Takeaways

- The entrepreneurial journey is a lifelong adventure, filled with challenges and opportunities for growth.

- Successful entrepreneurs are driven by passion, perseverance, and a growth mindset.
- Maintaining motivation and staying focused require setting clear goals, breaking down tasks, surrounding yourself with positivity, celebrating wins, practicing self-care, embracing setbacks, cultivating gratitude, and connecting with your purpose.
- Continuous learning and growth are essential for adapting to a changing world and achieving long-term success.
- Foster a lifelong learning mindset by reading, attending events, taking courses, seeking mentors, experimenting, and embracing curiosity.

Actionable Steps

- Write down your goals and create a vision board or visualization practice.
- Break down your big goals into smaller, actionable steps.
- Identify positive and supportive people in your life and connect with them regularly.
- Celebrate your wins, no matter how small.
- Schedule time for self-care and prioritize your well-being.
- Reflect on setbacks and extract valuable lessons.
- Cultivate gratitude and focus on the positive aspects of your journey.

- Connect with your deeper purpose and let it fuel your motivation.
- Commit to lifelong learning and growth through reading, attending events, taking courses, seeking mentors, and experimenting.

Remember, the journey of a Wealth Warrior is not about reaching a final destination. It's about embracing the process, learning and growing along the way, and making a meaningful impact on the world. So, keep your mindset strong, your spirit ignited, and your eyes on the horizon. The best is yet to come!

Recap the Key Takeaways: Reiterate the core principles and action steps for building a successful side hustle.

Inspire Action: Empower readers to take the first step towards their dreams.

Call to Community: Invite readers to join an online community or forum for continued support and collaboration.

Unique Elements to Consider:

Interactive Worksheets and Templates: Include practical exercises and templates throughout the book to help readers implement the strategies.

"Weekend Warrior Challenges": Offer mini-challenges at the end of each chapter to encourage action and track progress.

Real-Life Examples and Case Studies: Showcase inspiring stories of individuals who built successful side hustles using the book's principles.

Humor and Relatable Anecdotes: Infuse your personality and storytelling skills to make the content engaging and enjoyable.

Conclusion: Unleashing Your Inner Wealth Warrior

As we reach the end of our journey together, Wealth Warrior, let's take a moment to reflect on the transformative power of a growth mindset and the practical steps we've explored for building a successful side hustle.

Recap the Key Takeaways

Throughout this book, we've delved into the core principles that underpin entrepreneurial success. We've learned that:

- **Mindset Matters:** A growth mindset, characterized by a belief in your ability to learn and grow, is essential for overcoming challenges and achieving your goals.

- **Your Unique Value Proposition:** Understanding your strengths, weaknesses, opportunities, and threats, as well as identifying your ideal target audience, allows you to craft a compelling value proposition that sets you apart from the competition.
- **Idea Validation:** Testing your assumptions and gathering feedback early on ensures you're building a business with genuine market demand.
- **Finding Your First Customers:** Leveraging social media, building relationships, and creating compelling offers are key to attracting your initial customers.
- **Scaling and Automating:** Embracing technology and outsourcing can streamline your operations and free up your time to focus on strategic growth.
- **Financial Management:** Mastering basic accounting principles, choosing the right business structure, and practicing sound financial planning are crucial for long-term success.
- **The Entrepreneurial Journey:** It's a continuous path of learning, growth, and resilience. Embrace challenges, celebrate wins, and never stop striving for your full potential.

Inspire Action

Now, Wealth Warrior, it's time to take action. The world is waiting for your unique contribution. Don't let fear or self-doubt hold you back. Embrace the growth mindset, tap into your passion, and unleash your entrepreneurial spirit.

Remember, every successful entrepreneur started where you are now – with an idea and a dream. The difference is that they took action. They dared to step outside their comfort zone, face their fears, and pursue their vision with unwavering determination.

You have the power to create the life you desire. You have the potential to build a thriving business, achieve financial freedom, and make a positive impact on the world. But it all starts with taking that first step.

So, what are you waiting for?

Call to Community

The entrepreneurial journey can be both exhilarating and challenging. It's a path best traveled with a supportive community by your side. Connect with like-minded individuals, share your experiences, and learn from each other's successes and setbacks.

Join online forums, attend networking events, and seek out mentors who can offer guidance and encouragement. Remember, you're not alone in this journey. There's a whole community of Wealth Warriors ready to cheer you on and support you every step of the way.

Together, we can create a movement of empowered entrepreneurs who are building businesses, achieving their dreams, and making a positive impact on the world.

Final Thoughts

As we conclude this book, I want to leave you with one final thought: You have the power to create the life you desire. Embrace your entrepreneurial spirit, cultivate a growth mindset, and never give up on your dreams.

The path to financial freedom and fulfillment may not always be easy, but it's undoubtedly worth it. So, go forth, Wealth Warrior, and build the life you've always imagined! The world is waiting for your unique contribution.

Remember:

- **Embrace challenges:** They are opportunities for growth.
- **Celebrate your wins:** Every step forward is a victory.
- **Never give up:** Perseverance is key to achieving your dreams.

- **Connect with your community:** You're not alone in this journey.
- **Make a positive impact:** Use your business to make the world a better place.

Now, go out there and unleash your inner Wealth Warrior! The future is yours to create.

Actionable Steps:

- Review the key takeaways from each chapter and create a personalized action plan for your business.
- Join an online community or forum for entrepreneurs to connect with like-minded individuals and receive support.
- Continue learning and growing by reading books, attending events, and seeking out mentors.
- Celebrate your progress and share your successes with your community.
- Most importantly, take action and start building your dream business today!

I believe in you, Wealth Warrior. Now go out there and conquer the world!

www.ingramcontent.com/pod-product-compliance
Lightning Source LLC
Chambersburg PA
CBHW071957210526
45479CB00003B/966